SURVIVE & THRIVE

*The **MSP** Owners Guide to **Surviving** & **Thriving** in **Uncertain Times***

NIGEL MOORE

COPYRIGHT

Who the heck wrote this thing?

Copyright © 2020 by Nigel Moore

PUBLISHER

Who's managing and distributing this thing?

TEETH Group Pty Ltd T/As The Tech Tribe PO Box 150 Pyrmont NSW 2009 AUSTRALIA

DISCLAIMER

We care, but you're responsible!

CONTENTS

GRAB NIGELS BOOK

Head to **thetechtribe.com/book** to grab a copy of my book **Package Price Profit** where I lead you through the crazy world of working out how to price and package your MSP plans for maximum profitability and scalability.

"*I've heard there's going to be a*

RECESSION.

and I've decided not to

PARTICIPATE"

—Walt Disney

OPEN LETTER FROM NIGEL

Wow. Seriously Wow!

As I'm writing this, the world is a few weeks into the global COVID-19 pandemic.

And the resulting economic chaos and ripples. It's horrible to see the crisis unfold.

I've been telling my Tech Tribe members for a while that we are getting close to some sort of market correction (and perhaps a recession).

However, I had *no idea* that it would be this sudden or violent.

Earlier this week, I was on a panel with *Gary Pica* (if you don't know Gary, he's been one of the main thought leaders in the MSP Industry for the past decade).

And, during the panel, Gary predicted that once we get through this initial COVID-19 situation, that the MSP industry will start one of the biggest transitions or movements it's ever seen.

And, I completely agree.

If a business didn't feel supported through this situation, then as soon as they come out the other side, they're going to start looking around for an MSP to change to that they feel much more supported by.

Because, small businesses around the world will be taking their Technology far more seriously after this.

And, if they don't believe their current MSP or IT Support business is doing a great job, they'll go searching for another one.

The MSPs that show leadership, strength and thought leadership through these current times are going to be the ones they move to.

That means that over the next 12-24 months, there are going to be MSPs who will lose a lot of clients and there are going to be MSPs who gain a lot of clients.

And because you're reading this guide—this will help you to be one of the MSPs who stands to gain a lot of clients (and from here on in, I'm going to call you one of the **Winners** and the MSPs who are going to stick their heads in the sand and not change, the **Losers**).

In the last week alone, I've spoken and presented to hundreds and hundreds of MSPs on panels and group calls with other MSP industry experts like Gary Pica, Richard Tubb,

Todd Kane, Jim Stackhouse, Jamie Warner, Andrew Moon and more.

I've been asked SO many great questions.

I've heard some amazing wins.

Like the MSP who added 300 new leads overnight.

And, I've also heard some (heartbreaking) stories.

Like the poor MSP who was niched to the Travel Industry and 80% of his clients are currently shutdown and he's very worried he won't make it through.

So—this guide is my efforts to distil everything I've seen and heard and coached on into one simple document to help give you the best chance of being one of the MSPs that is not only going to **SURVIVE** through this period, but is going to **THRIVE.**

TWO PARTS

There's 2 parts to this current global situation.

SURVIVING—getting through the next few weeks (and perhaps months).

And, then what comes after. When it's time to **THRIVE.**

I've split this guide into those 2 sections.

So—put aside about 30-60 minutes and read this guide in full. It could mean the difference between whether you survive or not.

As a final note before we get into the meat of things, I love this analogy that my friend Mike Rhodes shared recently, reportedly originally from the consulting firm **Bain & Co**:

> *Think of a recession as a* ***sharp curve*** *on an auto racetrack—it's the best place to pass competitors, but it requires* ***more skill*** *than straightaways.*
>
> *The* ***best*** *drivers apply the brakes just ahead of the curve (they take out excess unnecessary costs), they turn hard toward the apex of the curve (identify the short list of projects that will form the next business model), and they accelerate hard out of the curve (spend and hire* ***before*** *markets have rebounded).*

The first section (**SURVIVE**) is your guide to slowing down *before* the curve. It's your blueprint for the immediate steps you can take.

The second section (**THRIVE**) is your guide for the *acceleration* out of the curve. It's your blueprint to come out of this thing cooking with gas.

I wish you, your family and your team the utmost safety and success getting through this craziness.

And, I'm looking forward to seeing you on the flip side, rip roaring and ready accelerate out of the curve!

Stay safe,

**NIGEL
MOORE**

p.s. I've scattered a few minor advertisements throughout this book that show you how to get more help from me and my business. I hope you don't mind 😊

SECTION 1:

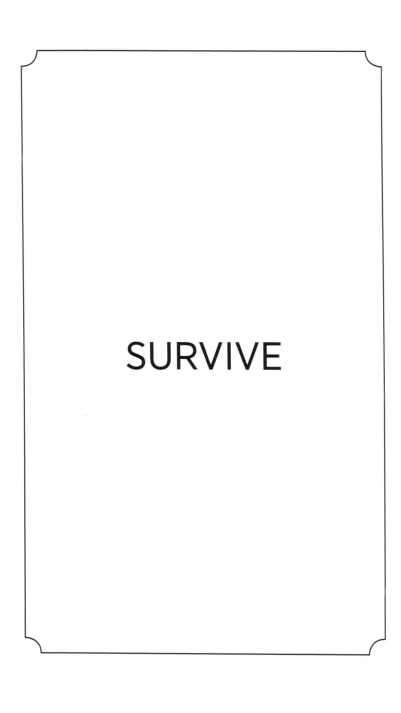

SURVIVE

COMMUNICATION

How you show-up and communicate during times of crisis is one of the most important leading indicators as to whether you're going to be a Winner or Loser out the other side.

So let's run through all the different types of communication you can and should be considering right now.

COMMUNICATING WITH YOURSELF

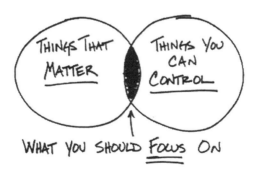

Now, you might be thinking why the heck do I have "COMMUNICATING WITH YOURSELF" in here. Especially first.

Well, it's because, the way you communicate with yourself right now will be one of the MAIN indicators as to how easily you will get through these uncertain times.

As they say at the beginning of every single flight...

You need to put your own oxygen mask on first, before you can help others.

And, the best way to put your own oxygen mask on first, is to make sure that you're operating clearly and calmly and communicating with yourself in a positive and realistic manner.

The MSPs that make panic, uninformed, irrational, fear-based decisions are going to also be the ones that will likely not make it through these uncertain times.

And the ones that keep a calm head and strong leadership in the middle of the crisis will absolutely have the best chance of not only surviving, but very like thriving through this situation.

Because, the COVID-19 situation & economic ripples is not the problem here. How you think about the problem is the problem.

Read that last paragraph again 😄

STOCKDALE PARADOX

I was talking to one of our Tech Tribe members, a guy called David, recently and in the conversation he reminded me of a concept called the *Stockdale Paradox*.

Jim Collins coined the concept in his amazing book, *Good to Great* and it's from a story about United States Navy Vice Admiral James Bond Stockdale.

Stockdale was captured during the Vietnam War and became a Prisoner of War. In the time he was imprisoned, his captors regularly tortured and beat him trying to gain information about their enemy.

Eventually after 7 years, he was released and returned to the USA.

Yes... 7 horrible years...

Many years later, whilst Collins was interviewing Stockdale about his experience in the Prisoner of War camp and he asked him "So, who didn't make it out?".

And Stockdale's response was profound.

"Oh, that's easy" Stockdale said. "The optimists."

Collins confusingly replied with "The optimists? I don't understand?".

To which Stockdale replied "Yes, the optimists. They were the ones who said 'We're going to be out by Christmas'. And Christmas would come and Christmas would go. Then they'd say 'We're going to be out by Easter'. And Easter would come, and go. And then Thanksgiving, and then it would be Christmas again. And they died of a broken heart."

Stockdale in his time in there maintained an unwavering belief that he WOULD make it out. But he maintained a realistic belief that he could be in there for some time.

And, my encouragement to you through this process is the same.

Be both Optimistic AND realistic.

Because, there are MANY lessons for all of us to learn through uncertain times like this.

- Lessons around our decision making.
- Lessons around procrastination.
- Lessons around confronting our fears.
- Lessons around comfortability.

Maintain a healthy dose of optimism that you WILL be coming out the other side of this thing.

Whilst at the same time a healthy dose of realism that it will likely take longer than a few weeks to get to normalize at our new normal that awaits us all on the other side.

Maintaining this balance will be the way to not only **SURVIVE** through this time, but to make sure that you make decisions and take actions now that set you up to **THRIVE** when the confidence in the economy returns.

FUEL FROM FEAR

There's no two ways about it—we will all likely feel some sort of fear throughout times like this.

- Fear of the unknown.

- Fear of the known.
- Fear that we'll look like a failure (you aren't).
- Fear that we'll let our family, our team and our clients down.

That's a lot of weight to rest on our shoulders.

And, so there'll be two ways MSPs deal with those feeling of fear during these times.

The first (and easiest) way is to run away from fear.

To stick our heads in the sand and hope that we can defer the fear. To jump on Netflix instead and worry about things until tomorrow, secretly hoping they'll disappear (hint, they wont').

The second (and harder) way is to lean into our fear.

Really feel it. Work out how it shows up in our bodies and become friends with it (yep, I'm getting a bit woo-woo here).

Once we can lean into our fear and realize that it's nothing much more than a few physical feelings inside our bodies, we can then start to use that fear as fuel.

Because there is incredible energy found inside fear.

Just look at our flight and fight response and how much energy and adrenaline it gives us in times of need. You can tap into that energy to pre yourself for thriving when you come out the other side.

Don't be one of the MSPs that succumbs to fear and gets paralyzed from taking any action. It's a slippery slope to bankruptcy. And even more so now.

TEMPER THE MEDIA

I want you to remember this...

The amount of time you spend watching the news and interacting on social media right now will be inversely proportional to your income levels afterwards.

Read that sentence again.

Not only is media a time-vampire.

More importantly, it's also an **energy-vampire.**

The more you watch it—the more negative thoughts that will enter your brain and start swirling around in there and clouding your decisions.

Sure, keep up to date with media so you can be on top of any critical updates.

Perhaps that's 2 x 10 minute sessions per day. But don't do any more than that.

Instead, invest the bulk of your time in giving value to people. Your team, your clients, your prospects.

The MSPs that focus on value creation now will be the winners out the other side.

And, I want that to be you.

YOUR COMMUNITIES

Now, this point might seem a little self-serving coming from me since I run one of the world's most supportive communities for MSPs (the Tech Tribe).

However, I don't want my bias to take-away from the point.

During times like these, you must lean **into your communities.**

Whether that's communities like our **Tech Tribe**, whether it's vendor-built communities, or whether it's just a bunch of other MSPs that you've built friendships with over time.

Whilst a lot of us are physically isolated right now, we shouldn't be socially isolated.

(I hate how they call it *social distancing*, it should be called *physical distancing*)

During uncertain times, you need to lean INTO your communities and peers and mentors. Not AWAY from them. We're all on this journey together and the more you can share your fears, frustration, challenges, dreams and aspirations with others–the easier your journey will be.

Get on regular Zoom calls with other MSPs, call your MSP friends up. Check if there's any group calls in your communities and join them. Get involved.

And as you do–don't be afraid to ask for help, share your struggles & challenges–because as I always say to our Tech Tribe members, **the only bad question is the unasked one.**

And, if you're having any wins–make sure you share your wins. It might be the inspiration another MSP needs to see to help them get through.

What I would say is to be careful in the free communities, as the quality of conversations, advice and negative energy that exists in them can nearly rival that of the negativity of mainstream media. Curate your inputs well.

COMMUNICATING WITH YOUR TEAM

Now, as I've just said over the last few points, your **Number #1** priority should be YOURSELF.

However, after you have looked after yourself, your **Number #2** priority needs to be your team.

One of the best ways to ensure you come out the other side of a crisis or recessionary period is to do whatever you possibly can to retain your team. Especially your A-Players!

Because, the last thing you want to do when the economy regains confidence is to have to be on the back foot to retrain a bunch of new people.

Including any contractors and close suppliers you work with.

In a time of crisis and with the threat of rising unemployment looking over them–your team are going to be in a very fearful state.

They'll be having thoughts like "Am I going to lose my job?", "Will our business disappear?", "Will I be able to provide for my family?"

And, they'll be looking for leadership.

Whether that leadership comes from you OR someone else is your choice.

So, right now–you need to make sure you're doing whatever you can to show leadership. It needs to be amplified in times like these.

RALLY THE TROOPS

Your team is looking for leadership right now.

They're looking for support. They're looking for positive news. They're looking for confidence.

And, you need to give this to them.

One of the first thing I did during the early stages of this crisis was to talk to my team both individually AND as a group to re-iterate a few things:

- That we're in a strong cash position to weather the storm as a business

- That we're also in a strong position revenue wise that if we had a serious bump to revenue

- The world will likely have a fight on their hands

- That whilst our business is important, Family is always Number #1 and if they need to do anything to help their family, they need to do it first.

- That our primary goal as a business is to help as many of our clients get through this as possible

- That our work is more important than ever now as our influence and impact could mean the difference between an MSP staying in business or going bankrupt.

If you haven't spoken to your team yet, I strongly encourage you to get them together to:

- Give them confidence that you're going to lead them through this.
- Give them confidence that MSPs by their very nature have some of the best chances of getting through this and coming out the other side stronger.
- Talk to them about your plan of getting through.
- Use the Stockdale Paradox of being optimistic AND realistic

James Eling, the CEO of a great Aussie based MSP, **Extreme Networks**, who does a LOT of work building an amazing team culture, shared his MSPs battle-plan online.

And, I loved it, so I'm sharing it here (with his permission) as you might be able to take some inspiration from it when talking to your team.

He called his whole team together (remotely and in-person) and ran through the following points with them in a presentation:

1. **Our Mission**—to solve small business problems. No change. Last week we worked to help businesses with productivity and profitability. Today, for many, it is surviving the crisis.

2. **Our 16-week goal.** Every team member retains their job and their house

(**Nigel's Note:** This is HUGE for team morale–they will all have a cause they can collectively fight for)

3. **Is it believable?** I shared the cash in the bank, receivables, the fact that we don't need to pay rent in the next 16 weeks and that Tina Eling and myself aren't going to draw a wage this month and probably not next month, so that we can achieve goals 1 and 2. We shared our cash flow plan for the next 16 weeks. We are lucky to have from financial reserves

    (**Nigel's Note:** HUGE again, showing true leadership)

4. **One-on-One's**–then we had One-on-One discussions to clear up any individual doubts.

PAYING YOUR TEAM

As soon as the COVID-19 situation started escalating, one of the first things I did was immediately paid my team some extra salary in advance.

I did this for three primary reasons:

1. Just in case there are any potential banking problems that would cause us to have trouble transferring money to them (or in them taking it out of their bank (just like in Greece recently)

2. So they have some extra money to safely stock up on supplies so they (and their families) feel safe. A team that feels safe will then be able to focus more energy on helping your clients get through this craziness.

3. Because my team are so darned important to me and our business!

Whilst other employers are out there telling their team that they might have to cut their hours or cut their staff, I'm paying my team in advance.

And, if you're in a situation where you have access to the capital—I highly recommend you consider something similar.

Whatever you can do to show leadership and inspire confidence in your team in the midst of uncertainty and crisis will be returned back to you ten-fold on the other side of this thing.

CUTTING THE TEAM

Now, I know I just mentioned that you need to protect your team as much as possible.

So, this might sound contradictive.

However, as I mentioned before, we need to be both optimistic AND realistic right now.

You need to do whatever you can to keep your A-Players.

But you also really need to be looking for who you might be able to move along IF and when you need to.

One of the silver linings out of a situation like this (and the corresponding market contraction) is that it forces us into making decisions that we know we should have made a while ago.

I know there's a lot of MSPs out there that have team members who really should have been fired a while ago, however since times were good and money was flowing, the MSPs didn't do anything.

If that's you—now is the time to give serious (and I mean) serious consideration to moving them along immediately. Because right now that could mean the difference between you surviving or not.

Plus, it will help you to protect the jobs of your A-Players.

If you do get to a point where you need to make some cuts—consider reducing the number of hours / days people work instead of completely firing them.

With high unemployment your team may be happy to have a 3-4 day week instead of a 5 day week.

Especially when their only other option is to join the unemployment queue.

COMMUNICATING WITH YOUR CLIENTS

Once you have "rallied the troops" and delivered vision to your team, then your next Priority is your existing clients.

GET ON THE PHONE

One of the first thing I recommended to my Tech Triber members is to immediately get on the phone with every single one of your clients.

Start with your biggest (or most loved) clients and just work your way through the list.

Check in with the owner. Check in with the Office Manager.

And simply ask them if they are OK and if they need any help.

Ask them what challenges they're seeing.

Ask them how their clients are doing.

Ask them what challenges they think might be coming up for them.

For some MSPs, this isn't possible for one person to call all the clients so they had to divide and conquer.

As you're having these calls with the clients, it would also be useful to just take a quick mental check of what you think their risk factor is.

For example, as you're talking to them and asking about things like their business and their clients, just take a quick temperature check with how you personally think they will fare through this situation.

Some MSPs I've spoken to have then categorized their clients in an Excel file in 3 buckets:

1. Will come out the other side Stronger

2. Will have some pain, but will come out the other side

3. Will struggle and might go out of business

Once you've got this list, you can then use it to start to make better informed decisions around reducing your risk. Things like:

- Should I tighten credit terms to these clients?
- Should I get heavy with Accounts Receivable if they are floating a big balance?

I've even heard of some MSPs who were negotiating with some of the clients to continue to offer IT Services in return for being listed as a **Priority Creditor** if the client slips into Bankruptcy to help them reduce their risk (more on that later).

And, don't stop at just one phone call.

Get back on the phone to them again, and again.

Make sure they're OK. Educate them on other things they need to keep in mind. Ask them what pain points they might be having. Offer them additional support and value.

I can't tell you the cadence of how often you should call. But, I will say that it should be more often than what you think you should. E.g. If you think it should be once a month for your clients, then it probably should be once every 2 weeks.

BRING THEM TOGETHER

A lot of your clients will likely not be used to working from home.

All since a lot of them will be business owners or management, they will be spending a lot of time talking to their sub-ordinates.

However, they will very likely be feeling lonely in terms of talking to other people at their level. E.g. other business owners.

So, one option I've seen some MSPs offer is regular Zoom Networking meetings for their business owner clients to jump on to share stories, challenges and travel the journey together with people on a similar path to them. You can be the host here.

Perhaps setup a weekly Zoom or Teams meeting where you invite all the business owners across your client base into a call.

Or if you have a lot of clients—run multiple meetings each week and invite different groups of people to each meeting.

Ask leading questions like:

- How is your team coping?
- How are your clients coping?
- How are you coping?
- What's been your biggest challenge so far?
- What's been your biggest win so far?
- What do you need help with?

Foster conversations and be the connector.

Your clients will thank you after this.

DON'T BE AFRAID TO EMAIL

I bet your Inbox has been filling up with millions of emails from businesses telling **YOU** what **THEY** are doing about COVID-19.

And, if you're anything like me, you don't care.

Because of that, lots of MSPs that I've spoken to have told me:

"I don't want to email my clients because they're already likely very annoyed with the amount of emails in their Inbox".

The thing is that you're not their HOTEL or their DRY CLEANER, you are their **MSP.**

Which means that they're actually looking to you for leadership in times like this.

So, my encouragement is to not be afraid to email your customers.

But to make your message stand out in the sea of sameness, you have to think differently.

This is a perfect time to ZIG when everyone else is ZAGGING.

Just like I'm doing with this **GUIDE**

So many vendors serving the MSP industry right now are coming out with bland, boring, generic ***COVID019 Remote Working Checklists*** that 99% of you aren't going to use or send out to your clients.

And, I've gotta admit—the first thought that ran through my mind was "I need to send a Remote Working Checklist" out to MSPs to help them.

The reality is though, that they are popping up left, right and centre. I must have seen 30-50 of them already. And, quite frankly—**they're all bland and boring.**

And, so my encouragement to you here is to NOT join the barrage of sameness that your client's vendors are sending to them.

Instead think differently and look for things of value that you can send to them.

A yardstick I like to use when I'm working out WHAT I should send is by asking myself the question

"What would my audience actually PAY to receive from me right now".

And in the case of this guide, I know that a lot of MSPs would happily pay for this right now.

So, instead of boring, consider things like these:

- An Online Workshop on How To Manage a Team Remotely
- An Online Workshop on How to Productively Work From Anywhere
- A Guide on How to Secure Your Business Data while Working Remotely
- How to Best Use Microsoft Teams for Virtual Meetings
- The Top Office365 Features to help with Remote Working
- 25 Cashflow Tips for <niche> to Survive in a Recession
- How to Reduce your IT Expenses without Reducing your IT
- All of these things are equally as valuable to send to Prospects as well as your Existing Clients.

CLEAN UP THE MESS

Once you've got all your existing clients up and running safely remotely, it's now time for your second and subsequent round of calls to them.

Because you shouldn't stop at just one round of calls.

Once they get themselves up and running with the bare minimums from home and they have a chance to breathe, they'll then start to realize all the smaller things that they need help with.

So, now is your chance to be their hero again and jump on to check in with how they're doing and help them fix up all the little things that are now bugging them.

Make them feel so ridiculously loved and supported that **they want to work with you and your team forever.**

TRAINING

Lots of people are learning a new normal right now.

Working from home when they've never done it before.

And, because you're in a leadership position in their world, they'll be looking to you for help.

There are some GREAT learning platforms out there that you can re-sell and re-brand that have specific training around Working from Home (WFH) including:

- Bigger Brains (from Chip Reaves, an MSP Industry veteran)
- Wizer-Training (I love how they make all their videos to around 1 minute for maximum engagement / interaction)

It's worth checking them out and offering them out to your clients AND prospects.

COMMUNICATING WITH YOUR PROSPECTS

Once you have protected yourself, your team AND your clients.

It's then time to get out and help your prospects.

I've been hearing horror stories of businesses waiting days–and even up to a week–to get a response from their MSP about getting them setup remotely.

And, as I'm writing this–every day we're seeing more and more businesses being *forcefully* transitioned to working from home.

So, there is a HUGE opportunity right now to help people who are screaming out for help WHILST showing up as their savior and good guy.

Here's what I'd be doing:

JUMP ON THE PHONE

The first thing I'd be doing is checking in with all my leads and prospects via phone.

Ask them questions like:

- How is your team coping?
- How are your clients coping?
- How are you coping?
- What's been your biggest challenge so far?
- What's been your biggest win so far?
- What do you need help with?

LINKEDIN REACHOUT

I'm sure you're connected to lots of business owners in your area on LinkedIn (and probably lots not in your area as well)

Well, now is a perfect time to reach out and check-in with them.

Remember, you have a cure and they might be screaming out in pain.

So, go through your LinkedIn and send all your business contacts a message like this:

✉ LINKEDIN SCRIPT EXAMPLE

Hi <FirstName>, Just checking in—are you and your team OK?

Do you need any help with this sudden transition to remote working?

Call me on XXX-XXXX or hit reply and let me know if I can help.

(don't worry, I definitely won't be pitching anything— just trying to help as many of our fellow humans as we can)

Stay safe,

Nigel

EMAIL CHECK-IN

The same goes for your email contacts.

If you have an Email List in a CRM, then great.

If you don't have an Email List, then I bet you a plate of pulled pork tacos that there are at least 20-50 business cards hanging around from people you've met at events.

And, I bet there's a truck load of emails in your Mailbox from prospects that you've sent out proposals to but for whatever reason they haven't become clients yet.

Now is a perfect time to check-in and see if they need any help.

Remember, you're not being predatory. **You have a cure and you're asking if anyone needs it.**

I'd strongly encourage you to reach out to all of them with something like:

✉ EMAIL SCRIPT EXAMPLE

Hi <FirstName>, Just checking in—are you and your team OK?

Do you need any help with this sudden transition to remote working?

We finally have all of our existing clients working safely and productively from home, so I thought I'd check in to see if you need any help.

Call me on XXX-XXXX or hit reply and let me know if there's anything we can do to help.

Stay safe,

Nigel

ASSOCIATION / LOB OUTREACH

Depending on whether you're reading this right in the middle of the crazy transition to remote working, or afterwards will decide on how much this makes sense.

Right now, chances are that *your* clients are probably running OK remotely.

But, there's a lot of businesses that aren't.

- Perhaps their MSP is so overwhelmed and doesn't have time to help properly
- Or, they only have 1 Internal IT person and that person is over-stretched
- Or perhaps they have been trying to do things all on their own (up until now)

You have a cure for their pain and need to get that in front of them.

One way to get in front of them is by talking to their industry associations and offering to host an online workshop and Q+A session for their members.

(this is an example of 1:M:M marketing–more on that later).

I saw a story from Robin Robins just a few days ago where one of her clients, Al, reached out to his local Chamber of Commerce and offered to run some online workshops around Safely, Securely and Productively transitioning to working from home for their members.

They agreed and sent out the promotion and he had over 300 new prospects join his email list overnight.

I'm sure he ran an awesome online workshop for them and I bet he now has a load of quite warm prospects in his list who's current MSP didn't do this for them.

Here's some example messaging you could use to get in touch with them:

✉ ASSOCIATION SCRIPT EXAMPLE

Hi <FirstName>,

I'll keep this short as I'm sure you've got loads on your plate!

Just quickly, I'm sure there's a number of your members who might be struggling with this sudden transition to working remotely.

We specialize in secure and productive remote working and have got all of our existing clients happily working remotely.

So, I'd love to offer to host a free online training workshop for your members to help them better understand how to setup remote working fast and securely!

There's no cost and we won't be pitching anything—we just want to help and offer value to our fellow humans in this crazy time.

And, of course if anyone is in desperate need of more advanced help, then we can have a deeper talk to see if we can help them.

Hit reply and let me know if you're keen and we can lock in a date/time.

Stay safe,

Nigel

☑ **ACTION STEPS**

Write out a list of ALL the Networking Groups, Industry Associations and Line of Business Vendors that you could get in touch to help their clients

Get in touch with them, ideally by phone or personal video first.

And then via email as follow-up.

COMMUNICATING WITH YOUR VENDORS

One of the bigger mistakes that MSPs will make during an economic downturn is to shut down, close or cancel their vendors.

The MSPs that pull away from their vendors and start cancelling parts of their technology stack resulting in delivering a lower level of service to their clients are very likely taking a big risk with potential severe consequences.

As I said with the raceway quote in the first section from Bain & Co, it's those who double down and work out HOW to deliver MORE value, not LESS that will be able to accelerate out the other side.

Plus, many, many vendors are offering special deals, discounts, lower prices, so there's a lot of help available for you to help you keep your clients.

And, the last thing you want to be doing as you accelerate out of the curve is re-joining, re-configuring, re-learning and re-setting up a bunch of tools that you cancelled too soon.

(whilst your competitors who didn't cancel tools are spending all that time marketing to your clients #toughlove☺).

CONSOLIDATE VENDORS

Now, I did just mention that you should be very careful about cancelling your vendors.

However, I'm not advocating that you should keep every single one.

If you end up having some down-time, it's a *perfect opportunity* to consolidate your vendors to standardize your Technology Stack some more.

For example, if you currently have two Anti-Virus vendors, with some clients using one and other clients the other–then any down-time is a perfect opportunity to consolidate them and cancel one of the A/V vendors.

This will put you in a better position when you come out the other side as you'll only need to train up on, support, and maintain one A/V Vendor.

The same goes for these types of things:

- BDR Vendors
- Anti Virus Vendors
- Telephony / Data / VoIP

- Firewall and Networking
- Cloud Vendors (do you have anyone on old Hosted Exchange platforms that should be migrated to Office365 still?)

OFFER HELP

Your vendors very likely have other clients who are **desperate for good help.**

This might especially be the case with vendors like your Backup vendor, your Anti-Virus vendor & your Telephone/ Data Vendor.

They might have clients that they work with directly who have Internal IT teams (no MSP) and are desperately seeking more help to.

My first recommendation would be to jump on the phone and ask them.

But at a bare minimum, you should consider sending them something like this:

✉ EMAIL SCRIPT EXAMPLE

Hi <FirstName>,

I hope you and your team are staying safe and well amidst all the craziness!

We've just finished getting all our existing clients safely and productively working from home.

So, I'm just reaching out–do you have any other clients that might need some help securely working from home?

We're not looking at making quick profits here–we just want to help as many of our fellow humans as we can to get through this crisis.

If you know of anyone that might be struggling getting their team setup to work safely and productively from home, just let me know.

Stay safe,

<Your Name>

You could also look out across all the Line of Business (LOB) vendors that you support across your client base (e.g. POS Vendors, ERP Systems, CRM Systems etc) and check-in with any of them you have a relationship with the same way.

ASK FOR DEFERRALS OR DISCOUNTS (IF NECESSARY)

Just like you want to help your clients, **your vendors want to help you**.

However, remember your vendors are businesses as well with staff and families and shareholders so **DO THIS ONLY** if you truly and honestly are in financial hardship. If you can still afford your luxury car payments and Netflix–then you likely shouldn't be asking for any discounts or deferrals because you're then believing that YOUR Netflix usage is more important than your vendors business that they've also likely poured their blood, sweat and tears into.

⊠ **EMAIL SCRIPT EXAMPLE**

Hi <FirstName>,

I hope you're staying safe and well amidst all the craziness!

Just quickly, we're at a spot where we're starting to get concerned with the financial stability of our business in the medium term.

So, I'm wondering whether you have any financial hardship packages that might help us have the best chance of maintaining business solvency.

We've not ready to give in the towel yet, so any help would be greatly appreciated.

Stay safe,

<Your Name>

IMPORTANT: If your vendor offers you a **DEFERRAL** (instead of a **DISCOUNT**) make sure that you plan to pay it when it's due. I've seen too many people take up great DEFERRAL offers and then forget that the money still needs to be paid.

REMEMBER: Your vendors are businesses as well, don't ask for help with financial hardship UNLESS you actually need it to keep your business alive. **Don't be a freeloader.** And, don't get disappointed if they say no—they also need to survive.

ASK YOUR LANDLORD FOR HELP

Most commercial real estate landlords are quite worried at the moment.

Especially since a lot of their tenant businesses that are being forced to work from home will end up realizing that they don't necessarily need to keep an office as big as they do when they return.

So, they'll be doing whatever they can to keep tenants now.

Perhaps, reach out to them with something like the below (please, please, please make sure you negotiate fairly as they have families and bills to pay as well)

✉ EMAIL SCRIPT EXAMPLE

Hi <FirstName>,

I hope you're staying safe and well amidst all the craziness!

Just quickly, we're at a spot where we're starting to get concerned with the financial stability of our business in the medium term.

So, I'm wondering whether you have any financial hardship packages or an option to defer some rent to help us have the best chance of maintaining business solvency.

We've not ready to give in the towel yet, so any help would be greatly appreciated.

Stay safe,

<Your Name>

DEALING WITH REQUESTS

A s I mention in the beginning, whilst you need to maintain a healthy dose of optimism, you also need to be prepared to potentially lose a number of clients.

Hopefully it's not too many for you.

Here's some questions and situations I'm seeing around the place:

SHOULD I DISCOUNT
OR DEFER PAYMENTS?

There's a few parts to this question and there's no perfect answer.

Like I mentioned earlier, you need to work out your risk factor for each client and make a judgement call based around that.

For example, if they're an Event Management business and after talking to them, you're really worried that their business might not survive and they ask you for a

DEFERMENT of all fees, you might be better off counter-balancing and offering a **DISCOUNT** instead so you can at least protect some short term income.

On the flip-side—if they're a client that is just going to have some short term cash flow issues but you are very confident will be around for the long term, you could consider a **DEFERMENT** with a Contract Term addition (it's higher risk but with potentially a higher reward [both in good-will and in contract asset value when you go to sell the business]).

DISCOUNT

Be careful with the way you position this if you are going to discount a client's fees as you don't want to de-value your work or give too much of an indication of your confidential margins.

Make sure you show it as a separate line item on their Invoices that shows something like "**Temporary COVID-19 Good-Will Discount**" so that they can see it and the value you're bringing them.

You may even want to track this discount to a dedicated account on your **Chart of Accounts** in your Accounting System so you can accurately track any COVID-19 impact in case that matters down the track with any stimulus package applications or accounting assistance.

Of course, if the client has down-sized and reduced staff, you'll likely need to discount / reduce their agreement (make sure your costs reduce as well)..

DEFER

Be very careful with deferring payments completely and only use it in the scenarios where you deem the risk to be very low AND you have enough capital available in your business.

Remember, you have hard costs (your staff, your software etc) and if you DEFER for too long, allowing your clients to continue using your services, you could be building a big potential debt for yourself.

HYBRID

Another option that may work in some scenarios is to take a certain amount off their monthly bill (perhaps 20%-30% so you still have margin in there) and instead of discounting it completely, you instead defer the re-payment of those amounts so the client still needs to repay them at a later stage.

You could defer the difference and then capitalize it in the contract at a later date, coupled with a contract extension.

Whatever you do, keep in mind that it will be remembered for a long time!

Also, realise that a discount from you is likely NOT going to mean the difference between them staying in business or going out of business. Their bigger costs like rent and staff will have a far greatest impact. **So, don't be walked over.**

EXTENDING CONTRACTS

With whatever option you choose above, you might also consider using the "contract extension" chip on your bargaining table.

For example, you might have a client ask for a 30% discount for 3 months to help them get through until stimulus packages kick in.

And, you might come back and say that you're happy to agree to that IF they are happy to agree to extend the contract term out by another 6 months to ensure the overall contract is profitable for you as well.

Again, you'll have to make a judgement call about whether this is the best option.

Keep in mind that extended contract terms will hold extra asset value for you when you get to the time to sell your MSP.

SHOULD I LET CLIENTS OUT OF CONTRACTS?

My default response would be:

"No, but I'm happy to work together to come up with something different that works given the unprecedented changes".

That might be a deferral, a discount, a hybrid or something similar that requires a re-negotiation between you both to find something for the **new** situation.

If the client goes into Bankruptcy then it doesn't matter as things will be out of your control anyway and you should become best friends with the Bankruptcy / Administration / Insolvency firm handling the matter (more on why later).

HOW MUCH SHOULD I DISCOUNT?

Tim Taylor, who wrote the great book ***How to Start and Run a Successful IT Company without losing your shirt*** (you can find it on Amazon) shared this great story and lesson in a community.

Right at the beginning of this COVID-19 issue, he had a situation with a client that was paying him $3,300 per month on a Managed Services Agreement.

The client has been hit hard because they are a staffing company right near the Disney parks (which of course are closed).

Tim knew that they'd come to him quickly to ask for either a discount or maybe even a deferment.

And, he was thinking they would want a 50% reduction in their bill and was worried about the effects of this on his cashflow.

So, he proactively spoke to the client on the phone, understood a bit more about their situation and offered to lower it by $500 per month and re-assess it next month.

They immediately agreed and said that the offer was very generous and they were very happy that he did it.

That's a LOAD of good-will he's put in without putting the sustainability of his own MSP at risk.

Tim's recommendation to everyone was to give your clients something (when asked) but don't over-do it.

And, that's my recommendation to you: Don't give away your house when a 10-20% deferral or discount might be more than enough to help your clients through.

WHAT DO I DO IF A CLIENT GOES BANKRUPT?

If a client goes into Administration, Receivership, Liquidation or Bankruptcy, your hands are often tied as to what you can do.

However, my strong recommendation is to firstly get your claim in with whoever is in charge of the proceedings whilst also becoming best friends with them (more on that shortly).

Depending on your jurisdiction and if you have the appropriate clauses in your terms, you might be able to turn up on site and requisition equipment (I've done this before completely legally, which helped us get some equipment that we could sell).

However, you need to speak to your lawyer AND your accountant here.

If, during your earlier triaging of your clients, you feel that one of them is likely going to go out of business BUT they still are screaming out for your help, you may be able to negotiate with them to be classed as a **Priority / Secured Creditor** in return for taking on the higher risk of continuing to support them.

This means that if they do go out of business, you will have a much higher chance of collecting your outstanding money than an unsecured creditor.

Speak to your lawyer to set it up as it can be tricky depending on your jurisdiction.

HOW DO I GET MONEY DURING A CLIENT BANKRUPTCY?

Unless you've somehow got yourself listed as a **Priority Creditor** (like I mentioned earlier), then the chances of you getting money out of a bankruptcy is very low.

If there's any money left over once the Bankruptcy firm pays themselves, staff and priority creditors, then it's typically only a few cents in the dollar (or pound for you British folk) left over for unsecured creditors.

The last time I got paid from a bankruptcy was 3c for every $1 owed. The one before that was zero.

However, I want to share a story with you for how I was able to find a **silver lining** in one of the client bankruptcies that was originally very close to sending me out of business.

And, it goes like this.

When I first started my own MSP, one of the clients I looked after was an amazing charity who employed over 500 disabled workers and created jobs for them in packing, sewing and other factory jobs.

(don't worry, it wasn't a sweat shop, this business really cared for their team and they had great working conditions)

These guys were a bigger client for me, sometimes spending up to $50k per month.

(which was a lot of money for me at the time, working from my dining room table)

The charity had started in around 1950 and was a not-for-profit organization with a seasoned board of directors.

In about my 2nd year of business, I received a call from the Office Manager asking me to quickly lock the CEO and CFO out of their email accounts.

"Oh–crap" was my immediate reaction.

Turns out, they had been forced into Administration (similar to Bankruptcy) and an outside Administration firm had taken management control of them and immediately fired the CEO & CFO.

I had about $35,000 in outstanding bills that they owed me

The administrators (bankruptcy practitioners) immediately called a meeting of all the credits and I keenly went along hoping for some good news.

What I saw in the room was chaos.

People were screaming at the Administrators at the front of the room. Tensions were flared. Fingers were getting pointed left, right and centre.

At one stage, I thought there would nearly be punches thrown.

The Administrators were doing their best to maintain calm and to explain to all of us their plan for helping the business forward out of this crisis.

And, I realized at that point, I had a decision to make.

Should I join the angry mob screaming and yelling at the Administrators?

Or, could I become friends with them and help them out as much as possible?

Luckily, even with all the fear and emotions cursing through my body, I chose the latter and decided to help the Administrators as much as I could.

I went back to my office and immediately built them a pile of things.

Like a complete IT Asset Equipment list, a list of my recommendations to help cut costs from an IT Perspective, an overview of all the business units from a Technology Perspective, a complete User Audit and more.

The Administrators were blown away at my eagerness to help them.

Especially considering I had just likely suffered a $35k loss.

They called me in and started giving me loads of work moving things around, cleaning up computers, splitting up departments, getting equipment ready for auction, sorting data and much more.

I ended up doing at least $30,000 worth of work for the Administrators alone over the next few months and whilst I didn't get my initial $35,000 back—this certainly helped me not go out of business.

As a silver lining, the Administration Firm then called me in to other Bankruptcies they were working on as well because I helped them out so much in the last one.

So, my encouragement to you is this...

If any of your clients end up going into Administration or Bankruptcy throughout this process, control your emotions and look for ways you can help the Administrators or Bankruptcy Practitioners do their job better.

It might just end up saving your business like it did me.

CAN WE USE OUR HOME COMPUTERS

One of the members of our Tech Tribe asked for advice on this one.

They had a medium sized accounting firm as a client who wanted to send all of their staff to work from home before they were mandated to so that they could be prepared and ahead of the game.

They were happy to allow their team to use their home computers to access the office network.

However, the MSP was pushing back and telling them they wouldn't allow them to UNLESS they were able to 1) Put their RMM tool on the home computers, 2) Update the home computers with all the latest patches and 3) Put their business A/V on them.

The client was obviously pushing back.

And, I completely get it from both sides.

The MSP doesn't want the client to be hacked.

And the client just wants to get up and running remotely ASAP.

So, my advice to this Tech Tribe member was that instead of not giving the client an option, they should instead **push the decision across to the client to make**.

And, to do this, they needed to help the client be able to make an informed decision.

Because if they kept pushing back too hard, *they might end up being the cause of their client going out of business* by not being able to get up and running from home.

If I was in their shoes, I would go to the client and say "Ok, so you have two options—each with pros and cons. Here they are, so you can make an informed decision":

Option 1: We let everyone use their home PC's without us monitoring / maintaining. You sign a liability disclaimer that you agree with the higher than normal risk you're taking in regard to security.

Pros: You'll be up and running quickly.

Cons: Heightened security risk. Increased potential costs to clean up security attacks.

Option 2: We quickly go through and roll out our A/V and Management tool to your users Home PCs and then they can access your network. Then they can access the corporate network.

Pros: Lower security risk

Cons: Slower to implement, higher costs for initial Out of Scope (OOS) work.

Then you're giving the client the choice and giving them the education so that they are informed when making the decision.

It's all about acceptable risk.

And, when you're talking to clients, you need to be using those words liberally so that they understand and accept that there's an increased level of risk.

It is *their* business after all and these are unprecedented times.

This particular MSP had the client's infrastructure protected pretty tightly (MFA and all that jazz) so whilst there was still some heightened attack vectors, their client is protected more than a lot of businesses out there.

CAN I CUT BACK ON MY SECURITY

This ties into the last question, however isn't necessarily linked in every scenario.

Right now, when you're having conversations with clients— there's no doubt that they're reducing their security left, right and centre.

So, the old **Security** vs **User Experience** conversation matters now more than ever.

I'd be talking to my clients about the increase security risks by discussion things like, in countries like Russia, there are high rise buildings full of groups operating completely like businesses, with CEO's and Account Managers and Team Leaders and Accounts Departments and HR Departments all managing and leading floors and floors and floors of hackers trying to break into you and your clients businesses.

And because Russia isn't showing much impact from COVID-19 (so far), these places are ramping up their operations like crazy as all they smell is opportunity.

These hackers are having a field day because a lot of businesses around the world have lowered their security drastically to get up and running faster.

So—when you're talking to your clients about the **Security** vs **User Experience**—really make sure you're informing them of the *increased risks* so they can be making informed decision over what they're happy to do and what they aren't happy to do.

SHOULD I SEND MY TECHS ON SITE?

In a lot of jurisdictions around the world where lockdowns have been enacted, IT Support has been classed as an **Essential Service**, which means that you're allowed to send your engineers on site.

However, that doesn't mean you should especially if there's a potential risk to their heath.

One thing I have been hearing lots more of is MSPs doing onsite work **after-hours** at client where there is no staff around.

They're stocking their team with the essentials like sanitizers, wipes and even masks.

However, during lock-down times, all non-essential work should be put on PAUSE and you should only look to roll an engineer if it's absolutely needed.

It's just not worth the risk in the most critical few weeks.

In the USA, I've seen MSPs making sure all their on-site techs / engineers follow

- Know the exact rules of physical distancing
- Are not sent anywhere if they are showing any symptoms at all
- Are equipped with any necessary items to protect themselves (e.g. hand sanitizer etc)
- Are carrying an official letter with them from the CEO stating that they are an essential service and that they're in transit for work purposes

STEER CLEAR OF LOW-VALUE WORK

I'll use an extreme example on this one to help make the point.

Imagine that you're a CEO of a medium sized firm with 150 staff.

You have a full-time cleaner on the team to help keep the grounds and offices clean.

Then, one day–along comes some economic turmoil and you have to cut budgets.

So you have a decision to make.

Should you fire the office cleaner and just get the team (or yourself) to clean the office.

Or do you keep them around?

Lost of people would fire the cleaner and just tell the team (or themselves) to do the office cleaning.

And, quite often, that'll be the wrong answer.

Because especially during times of crisis, you need to make sure everyone on your team (including yourself) is focusing on the highest possible ROI work they can.

Every minute they spend cleaning the office, is a minute they aren't spending growing or stabilizing the company.

And, as the CEO, the LAST thing you should be doing in periods of deep market contraction is getting back into the low-value work.

You need to be spending as much time as humanely possible on the highest value tasks in your business.

Things like strategy, growth, team leadership, marketing, sales etc.

So, as you're thinking about who and how to cut costs, also think about creative ways that you can do things differently

Instead of firing the cleaner, perhaps cut them down to 2 days a week and tell them to only focus on the basics.

If the office is a little dirtier for a few months while the rest of you save the company, then so be it.

A dirty office isn't going to send you out of business.

But not focusing on high ROI tasks will.

I encourage you to keep this mindset in every decision you make. You need to make sure you spend as much time as possible doing high ROI work.

Let the other stuff go for now.

MANAGING FINANCES

Cash is always king in business, right?

But right now—**cash is more important than it's ever been.**

Yet, one of the things that scares me the most when I'm talking to MSPs around the world is the high number of them that don't have their finger on the pulse when it comes to monitoring their cash-flows through their business.

If this is you, don't beat yourself up (just yet)—in my first few years of business, I had no idea what cash-flow and it nearly sent me out of business (twice).

If you weren't monitoring cash-flow weekly before, you really need to start now.

GET CASH

On a panel I was on the other day, Gary Pica (founder of the MSP education platform Tru Methods) suggested that any MSPs that have over-drafts or lines of credit, that now might be a good time to draw down on them.

Gary also went on to suggest to then move those funds to another bank if possible in case there is an attempt from the original bank to automatically claw-back (hey, it has happened before).

So, whilst I don't know your personal situation and your banking relationships, I will reiterate that **Cash is King** and so you should do whatever you can do in times like this to have as much on hand as possible.

The longer your runway and the more cash you have on hand, the better your chance of surviving and the more prepared you will be to **take advantage of any opportunities** when you spot them (more on that later).

APPLY FOR STIMULUS PACKAGES EARLY

Here in Australia, most of our (current) business stimulus packages are automated, so we don't need to apply for them.

However, in the USA (and likely other countries), the stimulus packages are currently being delivered in things like low interest, forgivable loans with no requirements of personal guarantees (SBA backed).

In the USA, there is already LOADS of CPA firms that are offering urgent **SBA Application packages** where they will guide you through the whole process for $2k and I've seen them closing 5-10 new deals a day across their client base. *(yup, that's $20k a day they're adding to their revenue which you might be able to tap into– see the breakout box below)*

You can imagine how many businesses are going to be applying for these, so my advice to you here is to stop what you're doing **right now** and get on the phone with your **Accountant** or **CPA Firm** and ask them for help with getting your application in ASAP.

The earlier the cash is in your account, the better.

You might also want to get ask your Accountant to send you a Financial Model of what you can expect (amount and when) from your stimulus packages as well so you can take those amounts and dates into consideration when you're making any decisions.

We are lucky to have a great Accounting Firm who proactively sent us, and all their clients, a **Personalised Financial Model** within a day of our Stimulus packages being announced, so we have a very good idea of what and when we will be receiving.

QUICK TIP FOR USA BASED MSPS

Reach out to your CPA Firm or Accounting Firm and ask if they have a **Fixed Fee SBA Loan Assistance Package** they are offering out to Businesses to help them get their applications in.

(Most CPA Firms are charging between $1,500 and $3,000 for this)

- **If they do:** ask them if you can promote their offering to your clients.

- **If they don't:** either suggest that they should do it ASAP (as their competitors are) and if they still don't want to, then look around for someone else offering them.

Then send a note out to all of your clients letting them know about the offering so they have an option to go to ask for help.

It's up to you whether you want to ask for a commission on any clients you refer across—keeping in mind that most Accounting Firms would likely be more than happy to pay you a few hundred dollars (or more) for any deals you send their way.

Remember that you're helping your clients here.

Because, getting an SBA Application in quickly might mean the difference between their business surviving or not.

CUTTING VENDORS

If you want to give your business the best chance of survival and give yourself enough available cash then, this next line might be the most important line in this whole guide.

Cut down on personal expenses first before cutting down on business expenses.

Now, I don't want to try to tell you how to run your personal life. Because, frankly, it's none of my business.

But my goal is to help your business survive through this thing.

And, since we've had a strong decade in a bull market, many people have added loads of unnecessary personal expenses to their lives. Things like extra cars, jet-skis, boats etc.

Things that you can easily do without.

As opposed to the Admin person in your Business, that you really shouldn't be doing without right now.

So, with all due respect—I encourage you to look to your personal expenses first to see if there's anything that can be cut or reduced, before you start looking for vendors that can be cut.

In saying that, you must also intentionally go through all of your business expenses and cut the fat.

Because just like we all likely made some crazy decisions on personal expenses during the bull market, we have also likely made some crazy decisions on business expenses during at the same time.

So, get your Admin or Accounts person to print you a General Ledger of your expenses over the last quarter (or maybe a bank statement/credit card statement) and go through it quickly, looking for completely unnecessary things.

Like the tools that you signed up for but never started using and likely won't be for the next 6-12 months at least.

Some questions you should ask yourself as you consider each vendor are:

- **Will this amount make a big difference?** If it's a small amount per month, then even the process of going through cancelling it, might not be worth the return for now–consider spending that time doing marketing)

- **Will this reduce my or my client's security if I cancel it?** Be very, very careful here.

- **Will this mean we're delivering LESS value to our clients?** As mentioned earlier, when you come out of the curve, you want to be delivering MORE value than before, not less.

- **Will I want to be using this thing in 6 months time?** If so, then it might not be worth the time to CANCEL and then RE-SETUP again in 6 months time.

(**SIDE NOTE:** if you're one of my Tech Tribe members–you're not allowed to cancel your Tech Tribe membership, haha. Just kidding. Although–if it's going to be dicey whether your business survives or not–just let us know and we'll work something out for you as part of our Financial Hardship policy☺)

MONITOR CASHFLOW LIKE A HAWK

Right now, at a minimum, you should be monitoring your cash flow weekly.

If not daily.

And, I don't mean just watching your bank account because that's a fool's errand and has caught many an MSP Business owner out thinking that Cash at Bank is an indicator of Business Health.

I recommend at a minimum tracking on a spreadsheet:

- All your Bank Balances
- Your Accounts Receivable Balance
- All your Credit Card Balances
- Your Tax Liability Balances (Payroll, State Tax, GST etc)
- Your Accounts Payable Balance

And, more importantly—I recommend tracking these *historically* with graphs so that you can spot trends. Quickly.

When I owned my MSP, every Monday my Finance Manager would send me an updated spreadsheet that listed out all of the above (and a few other numbers, like allowances for payroll & rent pre-filled).

This report really helped me keep a finger on the pulse of our cash-flow.

We had some fancy graphs in there as well so we could spot trends well in advance of them becoming problems.

And, a few times we had to make some decisions based on seeing some trends to make sure we didn't get hit with a cash-flow crunch. (personally for me, this Excel file was better than the cash-flow reports in our Accounting System as we had all our graphs etc in there to model and build scenarios with)

If you're not doing something like that currently—then please, please, please start the process this week.

Your bookkeeper, financial accountant or even an Admin person on your team can and should do this (you shouldn't).

GRAB NIGELS BOOK

Head to **thetechtribe.com/book** to grab a copy of my book **Package Price Profit** where I lead you through the crazy world of working out how to price and package your MSP plans for maximum profitability and scalability.

ACCOUNTS RECEIVABLE

Right now, the USA & countries are printing trillions of dollars (it's a conversation for another day as to whether or not this is a good thing long term).

In some way or another, a lot of that is going to be entering the market.

And, money will especially be flowing in the MSP space.

Even if we hit a global depression.

It will just become harder to collect.

So, I've got an entire section here in Managing your Accounts Receivable because it's such an important part of running a healthy business.

Even more so, now.

CHASE YOUR DEBTORS

Just as the squeakiest wheel on a bike gets the most oil, the MSP who follows up their debtors the most, typically gets paid the fastest.

And, right now—since Cash is King, you should be doing whatever you can to get paid the fastest.

If you've let your Accounts Receivable get out of hand (like a number of MSPs I've spoken to over the past week, who are all deeply regretting it now), then you need to start working on it now!

If you aren't comfortable chasing people up right now, then find someone who can.

There's plenty of great Admin and Accounting contractors on places like Upwork that are screaming out for work (and thousands more joining every day). These people would be more than happy to be handed a list and some instructions and to start calling your overdue debtors for you on an hourly basis (often around $20 per hour).

Just do whatever you can to get your A/R balance down and cash in the door ASAP.

Be sympathetic, not apologetic.

And, be careful to not be apologetic about asking for payment. The overdue money is rightfully yours. You shouldn't be apologizing for them being delayed.

MONITORING ACCOUNTS RECEIVABLE

On your weekly Cash-Flow report that we discussed earlier, you should now already be monitoring your Accounts Receivable Balance.

However, you should also consider adding one more number to that list:

- **Average Debtor Days** (the average number of days your clients take to pay)

Now, this figure on its own doesn't mean much.

But it becomes useful when you start tracking it historically. I.e. every week / month tracking and trending it to what it was last time.

And this will help you make quick decisions based on these numbers as you look at them each week.

When I first started tracking this metric in my MSP, our **Average Debtor Days** was averaging around 50☺

This resulted in some tight periods of low cash-flow.

Over a 12-24 month period by working on a pile of initiatives (some that I mention in the points below), our **Average Debtor Days** went down to averaging 10-12.

(at the same time our A/R balance reduced dramatically as well)

So, right now, you absolutely need to be keeping an eye on this number and do whatever you can to either keep it trending DOWN or hold it where it is.

And if you notice that it's continually increasing☺, you need to look at your Accounts Receivable process and tighten it up ASAP.

You need to become an even squeakier wheel, quickly.

That might mean that you:

- Increase the frequency of your follow-ups
- Reduce the time in-between follow ups
- Add some more human phone calls in the process (and earlier on)
- Put people on credit hold sooner (it sucks, but it's business)
- Swap more clients and services across to Automated Billing
- Sell more Pre-Paid Credit / Hour Packs (for **Out of Scope** work)
- Communicate with clients **WHY** you are tightening credit (so you can survive)

Again, ideally your bookkeeper, Admin Person or Accountant should be entering them this number into a spreadsheet for you.

AUTOMATE FOLLOW-UP

You've no doubt heard the term "The best time to plant an oak tree was 20 years ago. And, the next best time is now".

Well the same goes for an **Automated and Proceduralised Accounts Receivable System.**

The best time to set it up was 20 years ago. But if you haven't got one setup yet, then the next best time is now

Most of the latest accounting systems have features that allow for automatic follow-ups. And those that don't, there is normally external plug-ins that will do it for you.

So, I strongly encourage you if you haven't got automated follow-ups in place at the moment, then you should implement them immediately.

(you'll hopefully see your **Average Debtor Days** and **Accounts Receivable Balance** trend down)

Here's an example follow-up cadence you could use:

DAY 0: Invoice Sent (with either CBD or COD Terms)

DAY 7: First Friendly Automated Email Reminder

DAY 14: Second Friendly Automated Email Reminder

DAY 21: Phone Call with Friendly Reminder (and corresponding email)

DAY 28: Final Automated Email and Automatic Credit Hold

DAY 35: Letter of Demand sent from Lawyer (we used to use a law-firm who would send out a

Letter of Demand for a fixed price of $38. We only ever had to use it a handful of times but when we did, the client called within days to sort things out.

Sure, the timeframes there are quite tight.

But the reality is that by Day 35, the client is **5 whole weeks overdue**. That's a LOT of time for you to be acting as their bank.

(we used to use ConnectWise as our PSA which allowed us to automatically put clients on credit hold and this was great because it was "the system" that did it and not one of our team—it helped in the client relationship dynamic as we could "blame the system"😄).

Here's some example (humanized) email scripts you could use as inspiration if you aren't using automated email follow-ups yet:

✉ EMAIL 1-7 DAYS AFTER INVOICE DUE DATE

Hi <FirstName>,

Just a friendly reminder that the attached invoice is 7 days overdue.

We run tight credit control over here for two reasons:

- Firstly, because quite frankly were crappy bankers. And when we tried to manage credit risk we fail. We finally realised that we're not a bank (we leave that to the banking pros). Instead, we're your awesome IT Support business and we make sure to focus on delivering that!

- And secondly, we want to make sure that our business stays sustainable so that we are around to support you today, tomorrow and in the future.

Making sure we are in control of our cashflow is one way we make sure this can happen.

If you've already paid the invoice and our system just hasn't processed it yet–thank you and sorry for bothering.

If you haven't paid it–we'd appreciate payment as soon as possible.

To check out the invoice again–**click here.**

Enjoy your week and talk soon.

Regards,

<Your Accounts Person, Admin Person or Bookkeeper>

<Their Photo to Keep it Humanised>

✉ EMAIL 2-14 DAYS AFTER INVOICE DUE DATE

Hi <FirstName>,

Here's another friendly reminder that the attached invoice is now 14 days overdue.

We run tight credit control over here for two reasons:

- Firstly, because quite frankly   were crappy bankers. And when we tried to manage credit risk   we fail. We finally realised that we're not a bank (we leave that to the banking pros). Instead, we're your awesome IT Support business and we make sure focus on delivering that!

- And secondly, we want to make sure that our business stays sustainable so that we are around to support you today, tomorrow and in the future.

Making sure we are in control of our cashflow is one way we make sure this can happen.

If you've already paid the invoice and our system just hasn't processed it yet—thank you and sorry for bothering.

If you haven't paid it—we'd appreciate payment as soon as possible.

To check out the invoice again—**click here.**

Enjoy your week and talk soon.

Regards,

<Your Accounts Person, Admin Person or Bookkeeper>

<Their Photo to Keep it Humanised>

✉ EMAIL 3-21 DAYS AFTER INVOICE DUE DATE

Hi <FirstName>,

We've sent a few reminders already and I've just called your office today as the attached invoice is still showing as overdue in our accounting system.

The next step our system will automatically do is place your account into a Credit Hold status if the Invoice hits 35 days overdue.

Obviously, we would really hate for this to happen as this will stop us from being able to serve & support you out with any service requests.

So, please get in touch with us within the next 7 days before this happens so we can get it sorted out.

If you've already paid this invoice and our system just hadn't had time to process it yet–thank you and sorry for bothering.

To check the invoice again–click here.

Enjoy your week and talk soon.

Regards,

<Your Accounts Person, Admin Person or Bookkeeper>

<Their Photo to Keep it Humanised>

✉ EMAIL 4-28 DAYS AFTER DUE DATE (CREDIT HOLD)

Hi <FirstName>,

Our system has just automatically placed your company on **Credit Hold** due to the attached Invoice reaching 35 days (5 weeks) overdue.

We hate seeing this happen just as much as you do, so please get in touch with me urgently on **XXX-XXXX.**

The next step our system will automatically do if I don't hear from you is send this account off to our lawyers to start the collection process.

Of course, that's the last thing we ever want to see happen–so to avoid it happening, please urgently call me on XXX-XXXX.

To view or pay the invoice– **click here.**

Talk soon.

Regards,

<Your Accounts Person, Admin Person or Bookkeeper>

<Their Photo to Keep it Humanised>

MONITOR & RECONCILE PAYMENT DAILY

In my MSP and in my current business, The Tech Tribe, we monitor and reconcile payments into our accounting system daily (well, business days 😂).

This means I can accurately look at our revenue / cash generated reports any day and they'll accurately tell me what position we are in.

But, equally as importantly, this meant that all our **Automated Overdue Invoice Follow-up Emails** that get sent out to clients are accurate (so we're not annoying people unnecessarily).

Sure, there is a little bit of extra over-head, however it only took an Accounts Admin person on our team 5-15 minutes each day to keep it up to date.

And, the benefit of knowing that we'll be a squeaky wheel automatically, consistently and accurately was WELL worth the extra bit of Admin work.

So, I encourage you (if you aren't already) to Reconcile Daily and turn on those Automated Follow-Ups

START CHARGING INTEREST

Most MSPs have a clause in their legal terms that says they are able to charge interest based on a certain %. However, I've only ever come across 2-3 that have actually followed through with this *threat*.

Well, now is as good a time as any to turn a system like this on and start adding Interest to Invoices at the rate that you've already outlined in the terms that they agreed to ages ago.

This will help you become a squeakier wheel.

MOVE PEOPLE TO AUTOMATIC BILLING

Now, more than ever, is a perfect time to transition people across to Automatic billing (using things like ACH / Direct Debit / Automatic Credit Card subscriptions etc).

Especially any bad or late payers.

In times of economic contraction, it's typically safer to NOT work with bad or late payers at all.

So, I'd encourage you to alert your clients that you're switching everything to automatic billing.

And, if you get strong push-back from your bad / late payers, then you should make a very informed decision about whether you should continue supporting them or not.

Remember, revenue is vanity, profits are sanity but **CASH IS KING**.

If there's going to be a high risk that you won't receive the cash from them, then what's the point of doing the work for them with a high chance they'll harm your business.

If you have good paying clients that still want to pay manually— you should consider a **Manual Payment Processing Charge** (perhaps 2-5%) to help cover your costs and increased risks and to dissuade them from paying manually.

TIGHTEN CREDIT TERMS

If you've been in my world for any time, you'll know that I am not a fan of MSPs extending credit terms to their clients.

Because, there's typically no need.

As yet, I've never, ever, ever seen an MSP deal lost or won based on whether someone in the bidding process gave credit terms and the other didn't.

Most MSPs give credit terms to their clients because they *think* they should, without using any anecdotal evidence (me included for many years–whoops).

Once I'd learnt my lessons over the risks of providing credit, when it's unnecessary, I used to then always tell our clients:

"We want to be your awesome IT company and to do that, it means we have to stop also trying to be your bank. Because quite frankly, we're crap at managing credit risk. So, if you need finance, we're more than happy to work your finance company OR we can put you in touch with the finance company a lot of our clients work with".

I never once had pushback from this and I'm sure it's because of 2 things:

1.   We explained the reason **WHY**

2.   We made sure we delivered awesome IT support (this 2nd point is critical)

Now is a GREAT time to tighten up your credit terms because you have a great reason WHY (you want to remain sustainable to support them in the future).

My suggested Credit Terms are:

- **Managed Service Agreements = Cash Before Delivery (CBD)**: I.e. send the invoice a few weeks before the beginning of the month. It's due BEFORE the start of the month. This is if you don't already have automated billing.

- **Out of Scope Service Work = Cash on Delivery (COD):** I.e. the amount is due when you send the Invoice, so your automated follow-ups happen 7 days later.

- **Project Work = Cash Before Delivery (CBD)**. Or at a minimum, a <u>high up-front</u> %. E.g. 80% up-front, 20% with 14 days of close. More on that shortly.

- **Pre-Paid Hours or Credit Packs: Cash Before Delivery (CBD)**

If you feel like you need to go back to offering credit terms after this situation is over (hint: you likely don't), then you can label the credit policy change as **"Temporary"**.

CONSIDER WEEKLY INVOICING

If you're still offering Break/Fix work (or for any of your Out of Scope work for your Managed Clients), and you don't do it on a Pre-Paid model, then **consider changing your Invoicing Cycle to weekly.**

In the last 3-4 years of my MSP, we operated with a weekly cadence for invoicing (instead of monthly) and it really kept cash flowing faster.

It also meant that we could pick up any invoicing issues much sooner than waiting 30-60 days.

We also invoiced on a **Per Ticket** basis (rather than wrapping things up into a monthly invoice) so that IF a client ever had an Invoice Query, then they could only hold that particular ticket up and not the whole months work.

Where possible, I also encourage you to do the same.

If you're operating mostly with Managed Service Agreements, then there likely won't be very many out of Scope Invoices anyway, so this won't annoy people.

(and if it does–it might force them to reconsider jumping on one of your MSP Agreements at a fixed monthly cost).

The way the Weekly (Out of Scope) Invoicing cadence worked in our MSP was as follows:

- All time-sheets must be submitted before 10am on Monday morning (our time-sheets ran from Monday to Sunday to take into account weekend word)

- Our Service Manager than approved or rejected the time-sheets Monday

- Rejections needed to be fixed ASAP (we always pushed rejections back to the engineers so they could learn the lessons, rather than fixing the issue ourselves)

- Once all approvals are finished, the Service Manager notified the Finance person to run weekly billing

- Finance person then ran weekly billing (90% of the time this was on Tuesday)

- All invoices were then routed to a Manager to double-check

- Weekly Invoices were then typically sent by Wednesday

Sure, there were a few other steps to make this flow—but this is the rough guide in a nut-shell. It is worth considering something similar.

STOP GIVING AWAY SO MUCH FREE WORK

Now is a good time to re-consider how much free work you have been giving away in things like your Managed Service Agreements etc.

For example, you might be including things in your MSP Plans that should be getting billed as Out of Scope (OOS) work just because you want to be nice.

You might be rounding times down where you shouldn't be.

You might be giving skinny margins unnecessarily.

So, whilst right now in this immediate COVID-19 situation, it's OK to offer some free or cheap work as a way to immediately rescue people and build some long-term good will, it's also a great time to think seriously about your pricing.

FINALISE PROJECTS

Most MSPs I start working with have outstanding projects that have been sitting idle with an unpaid portion for many, many months. They typically just need a few low priority things finished on them to close them off and get paid.

If you have any of these projects, double down on your efforts right now to get them all closed off ASAP and billed.

UP-FRONT PROJECT TERMS

If you've been in my world for any time, you'll know that I'm a huuuuuge advocate of not giving credit terms on project work.

Yup, I'm talking about 100% up-front payments for project work.

In the last 4-5 years I owned my MSP, we operated like this on about 95% of our project work.

And, for the other 5%–it was typically negotiated with the client that they'd need to pay 80% up front and 20% would be due within 7 days (you could do more) of when WE define the project is completed.

That last part is important.

You don't want the client to define when the project is finished. YOU control the scope, so you need to control the project closure timing.

This gives your client 7 days (or whatever you define) to come back with any warranty type issues or steps that they believe haven't been completed so you can get them all sorted out properly as part of the original Fixed Fee pricing/scope.

Sure, every now and then we had a tiny bit of pushback, but we didn't lose a single client over it ever and once people got used to it, it just became the norm.

(the only people that normally pushed back were new clients that hadn't worked with us enough to build up enough trust that we knew what we were doing).

Over time, clients knew the process so well that they'd often come to us and tell us they'd pre-organised finance up to a certain amount and were ready to go ahead 😄

So, my encouragement to you—especially in times like now—is give out as little credit on projects as possible.

DON'T STOCK STOCK

If you've been in my world for any period of time, you'll know that I strongly recommend never keeping any stock (in most instances at least).

In the ~10 years I owned my MSP, we never, ever, ever kept any stock on hand (apart from the very bare bone basic things like network cables etc).

So, if you have any excess stock—look to either offload it cheaply (perhaps even as a big bundle of technology stuff) to get some extra cash.

And, then ask yourself the question:

"Do we really, really, really need to stock this again in the future?".

Because you very likely don't (especially with most distributors drop-shipping things now days).

One caveat to this is that since the current situation is meaning that there will be (and already is) global stock shortages, you might want to consider laxing this approach (but just temporarily).

CONSIDER A FINANCIAL HARDSHIP POLICY

Depending on your size and the types of clients you serve, you may want to consider creating an official **Financial**

Hardship Policy and subsequent **Financial Hardship Application Form**

(just like the telco industry does in most countries)

This would put a small barrier (or filter) up to weed out clients who just wanted to ask for a discount because now feels like a good time (not because they need it).

Your Application Form might just be 1-3 questions that you ask just to give people pause before they ask / apply.

It will weed out the people that don't actually truly need it.

But make sure that you're still keeping some "human" in this process. I.e. don't be afraid to still jump on calls and talk to clients about it–and if they ask for some sort of discount, tell them you'd love to help them out if they can just shoot through a few details.

Again, it depends on your size here. The smaller nimbler you are, the less an official process will be needed (the word *nimble* is an inside joke from my Package Price Profit book😄).

TAKE ON WORK YOU NORMALLY WOULDN'T

Now might be a time to consider taking on work that you normally wouldn't take on.

That might mean working with a micro 3-person business who you'd normally say no to–just to help them out to get through this scenario.

You'll have to balance up your capacity vs the potential ROI out of doing the work for this particular type of client.

IS IT TIME TO CALL IT QUITS?

As we wrap up this section, I want to talk frankly for a moment here.

And, I'm hoping this section won't apply to any of you reading this.

However, there may come a time in the future, where it's time for you to make the big decision and decide to shut down your MSP.

If you do get to that point, I have a few thoughts to offer you:

- Don't be afraid of making the decision sooner rather than later IF it means you might have some money left over to help you in your transition to the next thing

- Look around for other MSPs who might keen on buying your clients list. Sure, you might not get an awesome deal, but any money you do get might help you ride out a few months while you work out what your next plans are.

- Make sure you have good support around you if you do make the decision as there may be some tough emotional work you need to go through. Enlist the help of friends, family, other entrepreneurs and even perhaps a therapist.

If you do decide to close your business—<u>please do not feel like you are a failure.</u>

Because you aren't.

You gave something a go.

Building a business that is one of the tougher business models in the world to scale.

And, I bet you gave it an amazing shot.

And learnt a truck load of lessons ready for your next stage in life.

Be proud that you stepped up to the plate, gave it a red hot crack, helped a load of people during the process and had a pile of fun.

And, get ready for the next part of your journey!

TIME TO THRIVE

So, with that all said—we've now run through a pile of different things to help you as an MSP SURVIVE through the initial stages of a crisis.

Now, it's time to work out what types of things we can do to THRIVE.

GRAB NIGELS BOOK

Head to **thetechtribe.com/book** to grab a copy of my book **Package Price Profit** where I lead you through the crazy world of working out how to price and package your MSP plans for maximum profitability and scalability.

TEMPORARILY, DURING THE CRISIS, I'VE DECIDED TO DISCOUNT OUR TECH TRIBE MEMBERSHIP JOINING FEE TO THE LOWEST IT'S EVER BEEN.

Head to thetechtribe.com/covid for more details. You will have 1 month access to everything inside the Tribe (including all our MSP Agreements, our Training and our Ridiculously Supportive Community made up of over 1,000 users world-wide. We have no termed contracts so you can cancel whenever you want with the click of a button.

SECTION 2:

THRIVE

Right, now we've been through a pile of stuff to help you **SURVIVE** through all this craziness.

Now, how can you ramp that up and not only **SURVIVE**, but **THRIVE**.

Because right this very minute, all around the world, there are MSPs *thriving*.

- Like Ernest, one of the Tribal Elders in our Tech Tribe who has closed multiple new clients deals (over a million dollars worth) right in the middle of the crisis. **All remotely.**
- Or Leigh, another one of our Tech Tribers, who closed a 7 year old deal smack bang in the middle of the crisis. Remotely!
- Or Al, a client of Robin Robins, who added 300 new leads to his mailing list in a 24-hour period by using the Association Campaign I spoke about earlier

There are LOADS of opportunities still out there and here's where we're going to work out some ways for you to find them.

Now, if you're reading this guide and you've got this far, I can pretty much guarantee that you are one of the **world's best problem solvers.**

You wouldn't be running an MSP if you couldn't solve challenges well.

So, my biggest bit of encouragement to you is that this whole situation is to simply look at it as another challenge that you're extremely capable of solving.

Just like you do with technical problems.

And, like I mentioned at the beginning... I want you to re-frame your thinking.

So, instead of thinking "How can I survive through this?", I want you to start asking yourself better questions like:

- How can I THRIVE through this?
- "What can I do to make sure I'm one of the Winners?"
- "How can I give MORE value to my clients"?
- How can I help MORE people who are screaming out for help?
- "What could I do to add new Revenue streams?"

So, with those questions in mind–let's dive in.

MARKETING

SHOULD I STILL BE MARKETING

If you were a scientist and you had worked for the last 20 years on a cure for brain cancer.

And, you finally happened to work out the cure.

Would you then HOLD back the cure? Just because the pain that it's solving has a horrible context?

Heck no!

You'd be screaming from the rooftops–letting everyone in the world know!

Because there are hundreds of thousands of families out there SCREAMING for a cure right now for brain cancer.

And, <u>THEY NEED YOU.</u>

Now, of course–this example is a touchy subject–brain cancer is a horrible thing–I should know, I lost my Dad to it just recently.

However, I'm using it to make a very serious point.

Right now YOU have a cure.

And, there are a LOT of people screaming out for that cure right now.

It is your DUTY to get your cure into as many of their hands as possible.

Do not be shy in your marketing, do not be complacent.

Just change your messaging to match the current context.

WHAT SHOULD MY MESSAGE BE?

One of the most common MSP marketing campaign types up until a month ago is the offer of a **Free Network Assessment** or **Free Security Audit.**

And, you can bet top dollar that no-one cares about that type of offer right now.

It is NOT the time.

Instead, most business owners are in *information hoarding* mode right now.

They're stuck at home and are consuming content like no other time in history.

They're looking for advice, tips, tricks and strategies to help them survive through this period and keep their teams working safely and productively remotely.

And, so while they're hoarding and collecting information– you want to show up in their world WITH that information.

(just like I'm showing up in your world now with this guide 😄)

As I mentioned earlier, here's some examples of messaging that will likely work now:

- An Online Workshop on How To Manage a Team Remotely
- An Online Workshop on How to Productively Work From Anywhere
- A Guide on How to Secure Your Business Data while Working Remotely
- How to Best Use Microsoft Teams for Virtual Meetings
- The Top Office365 Features to help with Remote Working
- 25 Cashflow Tips for <niche> to Survive in a Recession
- How to Reduce your IT Expenses without Reducing your IT

And as you can see, none of it a hard-sell–it's all about leading with value and offering help.

The 4 types of marketing messages categories that will work well now are:

- Cutting Cost

- Reducing Risk
- Increasing Revenue
- Driving Innovation

BUILD AUDIENCES

Just in the past 2 weeks along, I've spoken to a number of my friends who all spend LOTS of money on PPC (Pay Per Click campaigns like Google Adwords, Facebook Ads etc).

I'm talking like $100k per month type ad-spend.

And they're ALL saying that their lead costs are dropping through the floor.

When they used to pay $5 for a lead in a campaign, they're now seeing costs of $1 per lead.

This is expected because there are a LOT of people making panic-based decisions at the moment to cut their advertising, so advertising costs on the platforms are lower.

So, right now is a good time to do some audience building while marketing costs are cheap. You might end up buying leads for 30-50% the cost that you used to.

And sure, they might not buy / convert to clients as quickly as before. But once confidence comes back and if you show up with value between now and then, they'll be the ready to buy soon enough.

Your decision here is going to be heavily weighted around how much capital you have access to and how much you're willing to risk it.

HOW TO THRIVE

You're likely going to hear a lot of people talking about the *New* normal over the coming few months.

And they're right–there will be a *New* normal once the main phase of this COVID-19 situation has passed.

However, in the MSP space, that *New* normal won't be ridiculously different to the last normal.

Sure, things will change. Some industries will suffer, some industries will grow, clients will make decisions differently, purse strings will be tightened in some areas and people will spend more in other areas.

But a lot of things will still stay the same.

MSPs will still help small and medium businesses around the world better use technology to run and grow their business and to innovate in their marketplace.

So, don't be fooled into thinking you must pivot your entire business 180 degrees and go off in another direction.

Because you likely don't need to.

Here's some areas where I believe MSPs need to be making extra effort now days to Thrive out the other side of this thing.

Some were existing opportunities before we went into this thing. Others are new.

CUSTOMER EXPERIENCE

Firstly, what the heck is **Customer Experience** (or CX for short)?

Isn't it just providing good Customer *Service?*.

Well, yes–that's a part of it.

But it's SO much more.

Delivering good Customer ***Service*** might mean that you respond to a client's ticket in a timely manner and you're friendly with them on a support call.

But a **good** interaction like that is not going to leave them shouting from the rooftops about their experience with you.

Because good Customer *Service* is expected.

But if you intentionally craft an amazing Customer ***Experience***–then you absolutely will have clients screaming from the rooftops about your business.

And you will create a client stickiness like no other. And get lots of referrals.

In my business **The Tech Tribe**, we have added hundreds and hundreds and hundreds of new members to our Tribe just in the past 5 months alone.

And the vast majority of them have been from referrals.

From Tech Tribe members telling the world about us on places like Reddit, Facebook, LinkedIn and at events and conferences.

Which means NO marketing dollars were invested to acquire 100's of clients.

How?

By loving on our clients by intentionally crafting a great **Customer Experience** that makes our existing members WANT to tell their friends about us.

Our Customer Experience is made up of many different things, like:

- **How we welcome new members** I personally record every single new member a welcome video using an app called Bonjoro—I'm up to 800 so far

- **How new members are onboarded**: We have crafted a short, fun video based onboarding experience with direct steps

- **How we celebrate their wins:** We have an internal process to send a little gift whenever someone shares a Win inside our Tribe to say congratulations

All of these things (and many more) have been crafted intentionally to create a great *Customer Experience.*

And, we're continually adding new things as we go because there's LOADS more Customer Experience improvement points we have in our back-log to add.

As we do this, we can't forget that we also still need to deliver world-class quality in whatever our core offering is.

For an MSP, that's delivering amazing Customer Service (not just good).

In our Tech Tribe, it's in delivering amazing training and templates to help MSPs.

So, how can you do it in an MSP?

Well, you've got to put your creative thinking cap on and work out what amazing touch points can make clients go "WOW".

The more "WOW" moments–the better your Customer Experience.

This can include things like:

- **Branded Apps** (e.g. Invarosoft–an awesome MSP Customer Experience app founded by one of our Tribal Elders, Jamie Warner)
- **Humanization** (Unique, funny, quirky human driven copywriting and messaging out of every piece of communication that goes out)
- **Company Culture** that keeps the Team Happy so that exudes across to clients in every interaction (read the book FISH)
- **Client On-Boarding**–craft an Amazing On-Boarding Process for new Clients

- **Client Appreciation**–be intentional about showing clients your appreciation. This might be regular gifts or even a personal video to say Thanks every now and then.

- **P e r s o n a l i z e d Service** (more personal than normal)

- **Unique Procurement**–yup, dare I say it–you can even work out ways to make your Procurement process fun. In our MSP, every time we installed a new computer on someone's desk, the engineer hand-wrote a note on a branded notecard telling the user they hope they enjoy their new PC

Over the coming 6-24 months, Customer Experience is going to become even more of a differentiator.

You won't be able to compete easily just by selling commoditized IT Support services anymore.

You need to intentionally craft an amazing, unique and entertaining customer experience around your clients interaction with you.

The more intentional you can be about crafting weird, quirky, entertaining, funny, helpful touch points into all your serious stuff the better.

☑ **ACTION STEPS**

Grab a copy of the books **The Cult of the Customer** by Shep Hyken and **Gift-Ology** by John Ruhlin and devour both of them quickly!

Then start adding steps to your Customer Experience to wow the heck out of your clients and create actual talking points!

BUILD ADDITIONAL REVENUE STREAMS

Most MSPs make the meat of their revenue out of the gross margin from their Managed Service Agreements and the labour from Projects work.

The margins from hardware and software resale are then the icing on the cake.

However coming into this new economy, you are going to need to investigate other ancillary (high value) revenue streams to add to your MSP.

This can (and should) include things like:

- Technology Education / Training
- Technology Adoption (this is HUGE)
- Higher Level vCIO Work
- Business Process Consulting
- Business Process Implementation Work

As I mention later on, these things mean you'll need to skill up in new things.

But you're lucky, because you and your team are epic problem solvers and so whilst these offerings and skills might feel unknown to you right now, with a bit of work and training–you'll be able to skill yourself up in them in no time.

Increasing your value to your clients and bringing more revenue into your business.

BUILD MORE PARTNERSHIPS

We all talk about it, but now is the time to really be ramping up the partnerships that you build with other professional business services.

Because, if you look out across your existing client base–it'd be safe to say that pretty much all of them would be using some, if not ALL of the following services:

- Telcos
- Accountants
- Bookkeepers
- Marketing Agencies
- Recruitment Firms
- HR Consultancies
- Compliance Consultancies
- Photocopier Firms
- Business Coaches & Mentors
- Education Businesses

And, if you look at your business right now, you have a big asset that is likely under-tapped.

Your client list.

Go and build reciprocal relationships with these people and create respectful and helpful ways to get their help in front of your clients.

Here's some ideas to get started:

- Online Workshops (e.g. a Marketing Agency teaching your clients about the latest marketing tactics)
- Lunch n Learns (when we're finally allowed to meet again in person)
- Simple Email Introductions
- Co-Promotions (e.g. for every Microsoft Teams Migration, our Telco partner is offering to throw in 60 days of free Calls)

With all of these complementary professional business service companies, you can either negotiate some sort of commission or referral fee for any signed deals.

OR you can simply just swap leads back and forth.

Although My preference is to always make these deals **commercial** because in 99.453% of cases where it's just a straight lead swap (i.e. you scratch my back, I'll scratch yours), one partner ends up doing FAR more work than the other and it turns out completely inequitable and therefor unsustainable.

☑ ACTION STEPS

Write out a list of all the complementary Professional Services offerings that your clients will need access to

---

BUILD 1:M:M PARTNERSHIPS

I was lucky enough to have once met the Founder of Xero (the Accounting Software) at an event and he taught me one of my favorite marketing strategies that resulted in multi 6 figure deals being sent my way.

He introduced me to the concept of **1:M:M Selling** (or 1 to Many to Many).

And, here's an example of how I used it to help grow our MSP.

One day, I looked across our client base to get an idea of all the Line of Business (LOB) vendors that we enjoyed working (yes, friendly LOB vendors do exist ☺).

And, I got in contact with them all to offer to take them to a (fancy & expensive) lunch to brainstorm whether we might be able to work together more closely.

One particular guy was the Sales Director for a Point of Sale (POS) vendor that we'd worked closely with at a mutual client.

I told the Sales Manager my team and I had enjoyed working with him and his team and asked if I could take him out to a (fancy) lunch to explore working together more and see if there were other ways we could help.

Being a fellow foodie, he accepted and we had a great lunch talking about all the craziness that goes on in our worlds.

Within weeks, this particular Sales Manager introduced us to a number of his clients where they were doing work and were struggling with the clients existing MSP.

We ended up closing on a few deals within weeks, that brought multiple 6 figures to our business.

Taking one guy out to a lunch for a few hundred dollars resulted in MULTIPLE 6 figures in revenue in our business. Talk about a good ROI 😊

I did that same process with a number of other vendors (the initial 1:M part) so they all then became our 1:M:M sales crew.

Here's an example email script you could use:

✉ **VENDOR LUNCH EMAIL**

Hi <FirstName>, Two quick things:

Firstly, I just wanted to say it was a pleasure to work with you and your team on the project at XXXXXXX. It's not often that we come across a software vendor that understands and appreciates the complexities of IT and that made it very easy for our team to work with yours.

And, secondly, I'd love to buy you lunch so we can have a chat and brainstorm about how we might be able to work together closer and help each other's clients out some more (we have some other restaurants we may be able to introduce you to).

If you're interested, does <fancy restaurant> at 1pm on either Tuesday or Thursday next week work for you?

Cheers,

Nigel

Write out a list of the top 5 vendors across your clients and send them all an email like the above (or even better, call them).

COMMIT TO A MARKETING CADENCE

If I was to run an MSP again today, one of the very first things that I would be building would be my **Network / List of Prospects.**

I'd be making sure I had them all in a **CRM** so that I knew exactly where each one was up to and all the conversations I have had with them.

And, then I'd be *committing to a regular consistent marketing cadence*.

That last sentence is SO important. Consistency in Marketing is one of the CORE principles, especially in our MSP space where the sales cycle is very long.

My cadence if I was to run an MSP today would be something like:

- **Daily:** Social Media Posting
- **Weekly:** Tech Tips / Education / Value Driven Email
- **Monthly:** Value Packed Printed Newsletter / Postcards
- **Quarterly:** Targeted Direct Response Campaign (e.g Cyber-Security)

And, as all of the above is **1 to Many** (1:M) it is missing some personal touch points.

So, for everyone in my prospects list, I'd also be creating a process to have regular touch points with **all of them** in a 1:1 personalised format.

The cadence is up to you, as you'll need to strike a balance between being the annoying over-enthused rep that doesn't give up vs checking in enough so they don't forget you.

For example, you might end up having some prospects on a 2 months 1:1 cadence because they're stuck in a contract and can't change for some time. And, you might have others in a 3 monthly cadence as they're starting to warm up.

Somewhere between 3-12 months would typically be the maximum amount of time for a regular check-in. All these touch points should all be scheduled in your CRM.

There should never be a single prospect in your CRM that doesn't have a future scheduled 1:1 check-in assigned against them.

I'd be mixing up the following regular 1:1 touch points types:

- Phone Call Check-Ins
- In-person Visit (if youre in the area)
- Personal Videos (using awesome tools like Bonjoro or BombBomb)
- Hand-written Postcards (I send truck loads of these each week)
- Email (although this is typically the last type of touch point you should use once you exhaust all the ones above)

☑ **ACTION STEPS**

Get a CRM in place if you don't have one already.

Get all your current prospects in there (people you have their business cards, people you've met at events, people you've sent proposals so)

Write out a Marketing Cadence that you can *commit* to (not one that you'd like to do, one that you can commit to).

Investigate the MSP Specific Marketing services to see what (if any) will help you out with this.

HAVE A SERIOUS MARKETING BUDGET

Most MSPs I speak to right now are wishing that they'd invested more in their marketing when they could have, so they had more clients, more prospects and a bigger buffer to get themselves through the current situation.

So, if you want to be one of the THRIVERS who comes out the other side winning, then you need to give yourself the best chance of that by properly investing in marketing.

As I mentioned right at the beginning, those racers on the race-track that come out of the curve in Acceleration mode start investing in growth BEFORE the rest of the market does.

Whilst there's no hard and fast rule or exact formula to tell you exactly how much of your revenue you should invest in marketing, here's some guidelines of percentages that I recommend MSPs invest into their Marketing Budgets (as a percentage of Revenue).

5-8%	MINIMUM
8-14%	GOOD
14-22%	HIGH COMPETITION / FAST GROWTH

So, if you were doing a million dollars a year in revenue–then at a bare minimum look to investing $50k–$80k a year into Marketing and Growth related activities.

If you're one of the lucky ones who has access to capital and you have healthy gross margins, then you might be able to afford up to the higher end of the scale at 14-22% of Revenue.

Imagine how fast you'll be able to grow if you invested that amount into Marketing.

VALUE FIRST PROJECTS

This strategy isn't for the faint hearted and is definitely more **advanced**.

But it's worth considering.

The way it goes is this...

Look out across your client base for opportunities where you know, with certainty, that you'd be able to help your clients either **MAKE MORE MONEY** or **SAVE SOME MONEY** by better leveraging and using their existing Technology (or new Technology).

Then, go to the client and offer to do the whole project for zero dollars up front and let them know that you *only get paid* once the client sees the financial gains of the project.

A perfect example I saw recently was an MSP who helped one of their clients reduce their Admin team headcount down by a whole person (which was costing them $65k a year fully burdened).

They did this by automating a process using existing tools from the clients Office365 platform (like Microsoft Power Automate) to move data between platforms.

This Admin persons whole job was to manually move that data from one system to another and vice-versa.

By delivering on this Project, the client was able to make that team member redundant (it's not nice for the staff member– but businesses naturally get more efficient over time– it's natural).

This particular MSP actually charged up-front for the work, and only charged a few thousand dollars.

But, the reality is they could have charged $10k-$20 using **value based pricing** AFTER they were able to successfully reduce the head-count.

AND, the client would have been more than happy to pay for it

(who wouldn't want to pay $10k-20k when it's going to save you a hard cost of $65k per year?)

Sure, this is an **Advanced Strategy** and you have to know what you're doing here.

But this is a strategy that works incredibly well during times of economic turmoil and in market contractions.

☑ ACTION STEPS

Spend 15 minutes in thinking mode (away from your computer) with a notepad in hand and think across all your clients.

Can you spot any opportunities where you KNOW you could make or save your clients some money by better using Technology?

Ask the client if they'd be happy to solve that problem for free up front.

CONSIDER OFFSHORE AUGMENTATION

Whether you agree with hiring offshore or not (that's a debate for another day), outsourcing parts of your business is something you should definitely consider moving forwards.

In my MSP, we had a small team of full time people in the Philippines.

> **Our Philippines team didn't replace our Australian team, they augmented them.**

We were able to get access to good people for one-third the costs of hiring people with equivalent skill sets locally.

And since a growing segment of MSPs are augmenting more and more with outsourced (often offshore) teams, **then you're going to need to seriously consider it in some way, shape or form.**

The way I first started back in around 2013 was by hiring a non-client facing Admin person for $500 per month Australian (about $300 USD) per month. This was for a full-time position.

Nearly 7 years later, that lady is still working from the MSP that acquired my MSP and has built a small team of people around her in the Philippines.

At the time, we didn't have the budget for a $60k per year Admin person locally.

However, hiring this person meant we were able to get a lot of repetitive administration tasks off my plate and our local teams plates so we could focus on higher ROI tasks to help grow the business more and deliver more value to our clients.

This first team member ended up taking over 98% of all our quoting and 100% of our entire procurement process (Purchase Orders, Sales Orders, managing distributors, Invoicing clients etc).

It took us a few months of creating SOPs and training, to get her up to speed—but after that, things worked incredibly well.

Sure, there are some complexities with hiring offshore, especially around cultural differences (I've done a whole training on this inside our Tribe), however once you work through them and get to understand them—life can be much easier.

And you can be freed up to focus on higher leverage tasks.

AM I TAKING ADVANTAGE OF PEOPLE?

This is a common question I get asked when talking about outsourcing, especially when it comes to offshore people who might cost 25%-35% of what a local person would cost.

The reality is that most of the time, you are giving your offshore team members a HUGE opportunity

For example, my team in the Philippines live very well compared to most of their friends, because we pay them quite well for their role comparative to local businesses.

Our Senior Developer has just completely knocked down his house and has a full-time team spending 4-6 months re-building him a brand new, luxury one.

He might not have been able to do that if he was working locally.

WHAT ABOUT MY PATRIOTISM TO MY COUNTRY?

This topic is debatable until the cows come home.

And, I completely get it from both sides.

The way I see it, is that I'm more of a globalist.

I love and deeply respect my country. But I also appreciate that I am just a human, that was lucky enough to be born in one of the most amazing countries in the world with abundant opportunity all around me.

And, I also appreciate that as a business, I need to innovate, be profitable, be efficient and find the best ways to deliver amazing to my clients.

In doing that, if I can help provide opportunity for someone around the other side of the world–then so be it.

You've got to work out where you sit on the spectrum here.

VALUE-BASED PROJECTS

In Chapter 9 of my book, *Package Price Profit–The Essential Guide to Packaging and Pricing Your MSP Plans*, I talk about Value-Based pricing and how it works with Projects.

If you haven't read it yet–then I highly encourage you to grab the print version from Amazon (search for Package Price Profit). Or grab a free PDF version: **thetechtribe.com/ book**

(it won't be free there forever, I have just set it as free to help during this crisis)

I won't go into much detail here as you can read all about it in Chapter 9 of my book, however suffice to say that there are truck loads of projects across your existing client base and prospects that will be screaming for attention.

And, if you can find them and pitch a value-based pricing model to your clients, you will find that there's much unlimited opportunity out there for this type of work.

This is stuff that'll require you to put on your problem solving cap and think at the vCIO level–but trust me, it's worth it.

Because, over the next 6-24 months there is going to be a HUGE influx of businesses willing to invest in IT projects that they've been putting off for so long.

NICHING CLIENTS

Whenever I'm coaching clients through niching, I always tell them to consider the downside of picking a single niche and how you can use hedging to your advantage.

(just like you would when picking a stock market portfolio).

when picking niches so that you can hedge your bets so that you've got some clients that thrive when an economy is strong and you've got other clients who thrive when an economy is in a down-fall.

And, the (admittedly extreme) example I like to use is if you focused on serving both **Construction Firms** and **Bankruptcy and Insolvency Firms** as two of your targeted niches.

When we're in a bull market, **Construction Firms** are normally thriving and **Bankruptcy and Insolvency Firms** are normally only doing OK to Average.

And when we're in a bear market or contraction, **Construction Firms** normally struggle and **Bankruptcy and Insolvency Firms** are normally thriving and struggling to keep up with demand.

So, if you're going to niche—be very careful that you're hedging your bets across a few different verticals to help shield yourself from any particular industry issues.

(like the poor MSP I spoke about earlier who put all his eggs in the Travel Industry basked).

NICHE MARKETING

In saying all that, I still strongly encourage you to niche right down to a specific vertical / industry wherever possible in any marketing campaigns that you run.

Sure, you can serve multiple verticals / niches / industries in your MSP and have many different niche types as clients.

But when you do your marketing try to be very specific in as many campaigns as you can. It keeps your advertising costs low and will mean you can get much more detailed in your messaging for that particular vertical.

Some of the most successful MSPs I know have specific marketing campaigns for when they're targeting **Accounting firms** and then different specific marketing campaigns when they're targeting **Lawyers**.

Because they can speak to the language of the niche in their marketing. They can speak directly to the Frustrations, Fears, Desires and Aspirations of that niche, rather than just a generic message.

And they're constantly tweaking, testing and adjusting them all for maximum impact.

In todays saturated advertising world—this gives them an advantage.

MONITOR AND INCREASE MARGINS

If you currently aren't monitoring your Product and Agreement Gross Margins, then you need to start now so you can keep an eye on them.

And, ideally as you're accelerating out of the curve, you want to make sure you're either:

1. **Increasing your margins** (typically by standardizing your product stack); or

2. **Stabilizing your margins** (by cutting unnecessary costs, or shifting to things like outsourced / offshore resources)

In Chapter 11 of my book, I run you through the basics of this. Go and have a quick read.

MERGERS & ACQUISITIONS

Unfortunately, the reality is that there will be a number of MSPs that will go out of business due to this market contraction.

There's no point sugar coating this because that's just the nature of the beast.

Hopefully, it's not going to be you (and because you're reading this guide–already have a greater chance of not only making it through this time of crisis and economic instability, but thriving through it)

Unfortunately, some MSPs will just shut up shop, close their doors and walk away.

Other MSPs will be forced into horrible situations like declaring bankruptcy.

And, over the next 3-24 months, there is going to be a LOT more MSPs for sale.

Businesses where the owner has finally had enough and wants to either retire or move on to other projects.

And, given this current situation and resulting economic ripples—a lot of them are going to realise that their business is not worth what it was before (sad but true).

So, they're going to be looking for someone they trust to look after their clients (who they've probably had for many years).

And someone who can look after their existing team and provide them all safe jobs.

They'll care less about the money.

Which means that if you're rip, roaring and ready to grow out of this situation—you should be on the hunt for these MSPs so you can work with them to come up with a **Win:Win** situation for you both.

If you have any in your current network, consider sending them an email like this:

✉ M&A EMAIL (ALSO SEND VIA LINKEDIN)

Hi <FirstName>, I hope I'm not coming across as predatory, as that's certainly not my intent. However with all this craziness that's going on, I've been speaking to a few MSP business owners that are looking for the quickest way out of their business and are even entertaining the thought of just closing it down (leaving their staff and clients stranded). And, if you're worried you might get to that point–I'd love to jump on a call and see if there's a way we might be able to help you avoid shutting down completely.

Sure, we might not be able to offer you millions of dollars up-front, however what we can offer you is a place where your clients and your team will be looked after with a deep level of care and attention compared.

Plus, some money to help you transition to the next part of your journey.

If you're up for a completely confidential chat–hit reply and let me know or give me a call on XXX-XXXX. Stay safe and wishing you all the best.

If you find any deals at the moment, you will be in a strong position to negotiate a 100% vendor finance deal where you don't have to put down any cash up front (or very little) and the seller is financed out of the ongoing profits of the business over a 12-48 month term.

If you wanted to go heavy on this one, you should build an entire targeted marketing campaign to send this out to hundreds of MSPs & IT Support businesses.

☑ **ACTION STEPS**

Send the Message out to all your LinkedIn and Email contacts that you think might be a good potential M+A target.

Follow-up with a phone call a few days later.

Follow-up again on a regular but respectful rotation.

SOME SILVER LININGS

Since about 2010 I've been hearing people say that the MSP Industry is dead.

And, I called bullshit back then. And, I call bullshit again now.

It's not only the strongest it's ever been.

But it's getting stronger. And more necessary. Every single day.

I'm a HUGE believer that the MSP Industry has a bright and strong future.

And, I'm also a believer that out of this COVID-19 situation and market contraction, there are some amazing silver linings for MSPs out there.

Here's my thoughts on a few of them:

CLIENTS FINALLY LISTENING

Even back when I owned my MSP (which was acquired in 2016), us MSPs were trying to get our clients to take things like **Business Continuity Planning** and **Secure Remote Working** seriously.

But most small businesses just hadn't been through a time of crisis before, so they didn't place any emphasis on caring

As soon as this initial COVID-19 situation passes—I'm predicting that the next 3-18 months afterwards there will be LOADS of work in these areas.

Sure, it means you'll need to add more skill-sets to your arsenal. Like vCIO stuff.

However, most MSPs I speak to know that they should be operating, much more at the vCIO level with their clients, so use this current situation as a good wake up call to finally dive in and get going.

This means, right now—you should be starting to think about:

- **What Skills & Training?** What skills and training does my team and I need to learn to be able to help clients with things like Business Continuity planning and other vCIO work?

- **What Roles?** What roles on the team can I plan to add that can consult to clients on things like Business Continuity planning

- **What Campaigns?** What marketing campaigns (internal and external) should I start thinking about as soon as we get on the other side of this thing

Luckily there's amazing tools like Managed Services Platform, Strategy Overview, vCIO Toolbox & My IT Process that can make your job MUCH easier.

Put on your list to check out those tools and work out what one might help you skill up in being a true vCIO for your clients the fastest.

EASIER TO HIRE

Over the last few years whilst unemployment has been historically low throughout the world, MSPs have really struggled with finding and keeping good team members.

Especially since we've had to compete against sexier industries like the fast-growth Private Equity backed SaaS industry etc.

Right now though, as horrible as it is, the reality is that there is going to be an increase in unemployment rates throughout the world.

Some experts are saying it might be up to 20% (or more).

That's 10's of millions of people all around the world that will be desperately looking for jobs.

So, one of the silver linings out of this situation is that it is going to become easier to find, hire and retain great team members.

And, with the influx of work that could be coming your way (like I spoke about before) you may need to grow a bigger team to keep up.

THE MARKETPLACE WILL CLEAN-UP

Like I mentioned earlier in the M+A section, there will be some MSPs that go out of business in a market contraction.

And for those of you Winners that weather the storm and double-down on your business, this is a good thing.

Because, coming out the other side—there will be less competition.

The good news is that a market contraction will typically weed out all the bad MSPs. The ones that only care about money and haven't built any good-will with their clients. The ones who haven't invested in security to keep their clients protected. These are the ones that will be weeded out.

FINAL THOUGHTS

I deeply hope that there has been some tips, tricks, strategies and ideas in there that will help you navigate through these uncertain times AND come out the other side in a better spot.

And, I want to reiterate a message that the legendary Rob Rae of Datto said publicly the other day and that's a huge THANK YOU to you MSPs.

You're the ones on the front lines keeping the many small businesses alive.

Your mission is important. Keep at it.

Because the world needs smart, savvy, funny, technology addicted entrepreneurs like you running MSPs. Especially in times like these.

We will get through this.

And on the way, we will learn some lessons and we will leave with some battle scars.

But mark my words, things will be even better on the other side of this IF you put in the work.

That's all from me—I hope I get a chance to see you inside our Tribe and hopefully after all this craziness is over, I get a chance to meet you in person at some sort of Industry Conference, Workshop, Tribal Dinner or Mastermind day.

Until then, stay safe.

Cheers,

JOIN OUR WORLD

I sent this book out to the Industry and haven't asked for payment or required your email address in return (most marketers will call me crazy, haha).

I did it because, right now, I care more about giving the MSP Industry some much needed confidence than I do about trying to get you to sign up to our email list.

I'm also a big believer in delivering truck-loads of value up-front, because I know that some of you will want to work closer with me in my Tech Tribe later on.

So, if you want to join my world and hear more from me, then you have 2 x options:

Join our email list at **thetechtribe.com/guide**

Join our **Tech Tribe** for the super ridiculously expensive price of $1 (whilst this COVID-19 situation is ongoing) and only $50 per month to stay a member afterwards (we have zero contracts so you can leave any time). You can do that at **thetechtribe.com/covid**

GRAB NIGELS BOOK

Head to **thetechtribe.com/book** to grab a copy of my book **Package Price Profit** where I lead you through the crazy world of working out how to price and package your MSP plans for maximum profitability and scalability.

TEMPORARILY, DURING THE CRISIS, I'VE DECIDED TO DISCOUNT OUR TECH TRIBE MEMBERSHIP JOINING FEE TO THE LOWEST IT'S EVER BEEN.

Head to thetechtribe.com/covid for more details. You will have 1 month access to everything inside the Tribe (including all our MSP Agreements, our Training and our Ridiculously Supportive Community made up of over 1,000 users world-wide. We have no termed contracts so you can cancel whenever you want with the click of a button.

Made in the USA
Middletown, DE
20 October 2021